A DICTIONARY

OF

ENGLISH PROVERBS

MJP
PUBLISHERS

A DICTIONARY

OF

ENGLISH PROVERBS

Thomas Preston

MJP
PUBLISHERS

Chennai   Trichy   Tirunelveli   New Delhi

ISBN 978-93-87826-15-1   **MJP Publishers**

All rights reserved   No. 44, Nallathambi Street,
Printed and bound in India   Triplicane, Chennai 600 005
MJP 446   © Publishers, 2019

Publisher   C. Janarthanan

Project Editor   C. Ambica

PUBLISHER'S NOTE

The legacy of a country is in its varied cultural heritage, historical literature, developments in the field of economy and science. The top nations in the world are competing in the field of science, economy and literature. This vast legacy has to be conserved and documented so that it can be bestowed to the future generation. The knowledge of this legacy is slowly getting perished in the present generation due to lack of documentation.

Keeping this in mind, the concern with retrospective acquiring of rare books has been accented recently by the burgeoning reprint industry. MJP Publishers is gratified to retrieve the rare collections with a view to bring back those books that were landmarks in their time.

In this effort, a series of rare books would be republished under the banner, "MJP Publishers". The books in the reprint series have been carefully selected for their contemporary usefulness as well as their historical importance within the intellectual. We reconstruct the book with slight enhancements made for better presentation, without affecting the contents of the original edition.

Most of the works selected for republishing covers a huge range of subjects, from history to anthropology. We believe this reprint edition will be a service to the numerous researchers and practitioners active in this fascinating field. We allow readers to experience the wonder of peering into a scholarly work of the highest order and seminal significance.

MJP Publishers

PREFACE

Long before writing and books were in common use, proverbs were the principal means of imparting instruction. In modern times there is not so much need to apply these old sayings as a means of educating the people, but they are still constantly met with in the newspapers and in general literature, and they are rightly considered as "The texts of common life."

The late Earl Russell very aptly described a proverb as "The wisdom of many and the wit of one." We value proverbs chiefly as moral maxims teaching some practical lesson set forth in concise, pithy sentences, which are fixed in the memory without effort, and retained without being burdensome. They have been found useful for guidance in almost every condition of life; but, on the other hand, it is quite true that many dangerous precepts have been propounded in proverbs, and some of the older ones gave such questionable advice, or were couched in such objectionable language, that they have been very properly omitted from every collection intended, as this is, for general use. Other old proverbs have become obsolete, and as their meaning is now obscure, they have not been included in the Dictionary.

This series of "Handy Books" would hardly be complete without a collection of English Proverbs. Many books on the subject have been written, but it is hoped that this collection will, in some respects, be found to be an improvement on all its predecessors. Like The Dictionary of Daily Blunders, this Dictionary of English Proverbs has been framed so as to enable the reader to find what he wants without difficulty. The Dictionary itself is arranged according to the principal words, and there is also a Copious Index of additional principal words.

Other modern collections profess to give an "Alphabetical Index," but such an index is of little use when we find that it is framed on the rule that because a proverb begins with the article *A*, it should therefore be indexed under that letter. As, "A bald head is soon shaven." In another similar Index we find the proverb, "'Tis the second blow makes the fray," inserted under the letter *T*. In one index of this kind there are no less than twenty-two pages of *A's* and almost as many of *The's*. Indeed the whole index is compiled without the slightest regard to the subject of the proverbs. On this subject Disraeli, in his essay on the "Philosophy of Proverbs," says "The arrangement of proverbs has baffled the ingenuity of every one of their collectors. Ray, after long premeditation, has chosen a system with the appearance of an alphabetical order, but it turns out that his system is no system, and his alphabet is no alphabet. After ten years' labour the good man could only arrange his proverbs by commonplaces." In this little Dictionary, as we have already stated, the proverbs are arranged in alphabetical order, according to the leading words, and are consecutively numbered. But, in order to avoid repetition (as most of the proverbs contain, at least, two leading words), the *subject words* are used for the Dictionary, and the other principal words will be found in the Index, with a numerical reference to the proverb. The great advantage of this arrangement is, that if only one important word of a proverb be remembered, that word can be turned to in the Dictionary, and, if not found there, will certainly be in the Index. Nearly two thousand of the leading words are thus indexed—enough to make it almost impossible to miss finding what is wanted. This plan has also the effect of bringing together the proverbs on kindred subjects, which is often a matter of importance to writers, and is, moreover, most amusing to those who only read the book to while away a leisure hour. Ready reference is further facilitated in the Index by the addition of associated words. If one word only had been given, the reader might have had to refer to eleven proverbs before he found the one he required; as, for example, in the case of *Dog*.

It may be convenient to state that the Dictionary has been compiled principally from Ray's collection, first published in 1670. The remainder of the proverbs have been collected from ancient and modern literature; but some few of them will not be found in any other published collection.

It only remains to remind the reader that this is a collection of ENGLISH Proverbs only; and we may appropriately conclude our Preface with a further extract from Disraeli's essay, wherein he very justly remarks that "The experience of life will throw a perpetual freshness over these short and simple texts; every day may furnish a new commentary; and we may grow old and still find novelty in proverbs by their perpetual application."

A

Absence Absence cools moderate passions, and inflames violent ones.

Absent The absent are always at fault.

Absent Long absent, soon forgotten.

Aching Teeth Who hath aching teeth, hath ill tenants.

Adversity Adversity makes a man wise, not rich.

Adversity Adversity tries friends.

Adversity Adversity flattereth no man.

Advice Give neither advice nor salt until you are asked for it.

Advice What every one asks, what every one gives, but what very few take—advice.

Advice In vain he craves advice who will not follow it.

Advice Advice comes too late when a thing is done.

Afraid of wounds He that's afraid of wounds must not come nigh a battle.

Afraid More afraid than hurt.

Age Age before honesty.

Age (old) Old age is honourable.

Agree Two of a trade seldom agree.

Agree Agree, for law is costly.

Ague An ague in the spring, Is physic for a king.

Agues Agues come on horseback, but go away on foot.

Air A man cannot live by the air.

Alchemy No alchemy like saving.

Ale Good ale is meat, drink, and cloth.

Ale He that buys land buys many stones, He that buys flesh buys many bones, He that buys eggs buys many shells, He that buys ale buys nothing else.

Ale-House Every one has a penny to spend at a new ale-house.

All's Well All's well that ends well.

All Things No living manAll things can.

Almost Almost was never hanged.

Alms Steal the goose, and give the giblets in alms.

Anger Anger is short-lived in a good man.

Anger Keep from the anger of a great man.

Angry Men Angry men seldom want woe.

Angry He that is angry without a cause must be pleased without amends.

Another's Burden None knows the weight of another's burden.

Apples Apples, eggs, and nuts,One may eat after sluts.

April April and May are the keys of the year.

April When April blows his horn,It's both good for hay and corn.

April April borrows three days of March, and they are ill.

April Showers March winds and April showersBring forth May flowers.

Argus Argus at home, but a mole abroad.

Ashamed Never be ashamed to eat your meat.

Ashes Every man must eat a peck of ashes before he dies.

Ask Ask but enough, and you may lower as you list.

Ask   Ask thy purse what thou shouldst buy.

Asking   Lose nothing for asking.

Ass   The ass that brays most, eats least.

Ass   Every ass thinks himself worthy to stand with the king's horses.

August   August dry and warm, Harvest doth no harm.

August   If the twenty-fourth of August be fair and clear, Then hope for a prosperous autumn that year.

August   A wet August never brings dearth.

Author   Like author, like book.

B

Bachelors Bachelors grin, but married men laugh till their hearts ache.

Bachelors' Wives Bachelors' wives and maids' children are always well taught.

Bad Where bad's the best, naught must be the choice.

Bad Company Better be alone than in bad company.

Bad Day A bad day never hath a good night.

Bad Market He that cannot abide a bad market deserves not a good one.

Bagpipe Bring not a bagpipe to a man in trouble.

Bags He is most loved that hath most bags.

Bail Be bail and pay for it.

Balance The balance distinguishes not between gold and lead.

Bald Head A bald head is soon shaven.

Banquet There's no great banquet but some fare ill.

Barber's Chair Like a barber's chair, fit for every buttock.

Barber One barber shaves not so close but another finds work.

Barefooted Barefooted men should not tread on thorns.

Bare Foot Better a bare foot than no foot at all.

Bargain Make the best of a bad bargain.

Bargain A bargain is a bargain.

Bargain At a great bargain make a great pause.

Bark What! keep a dog and bark myself?

Barkers The greatest barkers are not always the sorest biters.

Barley When the sloe-tree is as white as a sheet,Sow your barley, whether it be dry or wet.

Barleycorn Sir John Barleycorn is the strongest knight.

Barley Straw Barley straw's good fodder when the cow gives water.

Barrel You cannot know wine by the barrel.

Batchelor Commend a wedded life, but keep thyself a batchelor.

Bean Every bean has its black.

Beans Sow beans in the mud, they'll grow like wood.

Beans Beans should blow before May doth go.

Bear A man may bear till his back breaks.

Bear Bear and forbear.

Bear Bear with evil and expect good.

Beat 'Tis easy to find a staff to beat a dog.

Beaten Better to be beaten than be in bad company.

Beaten A spaniel, a woman, and a walnut tree,The more they're beaten the better they be.

Beauty Beauty buys no beef.

Beauty Beauty is no inheritance.

Beauty Beauty is but skin deep.

Bed As you make your bed so you must lie on it.

Bed He who lies long in bed his estate feels it.

Bees A swarm of bees in May is worth a load of hay, But a swarm of bees in July is not worth a fly.

Bees Where bees are there is honey.

Before He that hires the horse must ride before.

Beggar Better be a beggar than a fool.

Beggar   A beggar can never be bankrupt.

Beggar   The beggar is never out of his way.

Beggars   Beggars must not be choosers.

Beggars   Beggars on horseback will ride to the devil.

Beggary   Trash and trumpery is the highway to beggary.

Begging   Begging is an ill trade on a fast-day.

Beginning   A good beginning makes a good ending.

Beginning   Such a beginning, such an end.

Begin well   Good to begin well; better to end well.

Begun   Well begun is half done.

Behind   When two ride together one must ride behind.

Believe   You would make me believe the moon is made of green cheese.

Believe   Believe well and have well.

Bell   Fear not the loss of the bell more than the loss of the steeple.

Best   The best is cheapest.

Best   The best lie is the worst.

Best   Make the best of a bad bargain.

Best Dog   Let the best dog leap the stile first.

Bet   Any fool can bet.

Better   The better the day, the better the deed.

Beware   Beware of "Had I wist."

Bidden   Do as you are bidden and you'll never be to blame.

Birchen Twigs   Birchen twigs break no ribs.

Bird   A bird in the hand is worth two in the bush.

Bird   Every bird must hatch her own egg.

Bird   One beats the bush and another catcheth the bird.

Birds   Birds of a feather flock together.

Bird The bird that can sing and will not sing, must be made to sing.

Birds (small) Even small birds must have meat.

Bite If you cannot bite, never show your teeth.

Bites He that bites on every weed must needs light on poison.

Bit A bit in the morning is better than nothing all day.

Bitter Bird Thou art a bitter bird, said the raven to the starling.

Black Plum A black plum is as sweet as a white.

Blast The sharper the blast, The shorter 'twill last.

Blind As blind as a bat.

Blind Who so blind as he that will not see?

Blind Man A blind man would be glad to see it.

Blind Man Like a treatise on light and colours by a blind man.

Blood You cannot get blood out of a stone.

Blot 'Tis a blot on his escutcheon.

Blushing Blushing is virtue's colour.

Blusters He who blusters without reason has most reason to bluster.

Boast Great boast, small roast.

Boil Snow Whether you boil snow or pound it, you will have but water from it.

Bone Give a dog a bone in his mouth, and you may kick him and he can't bite.

Bone I have a bone in my arm.

Bone The nearer the bone the sweeter the meat.

Born He that is born to be hanged shall never be drowned.

Borrowed Garments Borrowed garments never fit well.

Bought Wit Bought wit is best.

Bought Wit Bought wit makes folk wise.

Bound They that are bound must obey.

Bow A bow long bent at last waxeth weak.

Bowl It is easy to bowl down hill.

Boys Boys will be boys.

Brag Brag's a good dog, but Holdfast is a better.

Brag Brag's a good dog, but that he hath lost his tail.

Brag Brag's a good dog if he be well set on; but he dare not bite.

Braggers Great braggers, little doers.

Brain The brain that sows not corn, plants thistles.

Bran Much bran, little meal.

Bread and Butter They that have no other meat,Bread and butter are glad to eat.

Breakfast He who would have a hare for breakfast must hunt over night.

Breaking The best horse needs breaking, and the best child needs teaching.

Bred That which is bred in the bone will never be out of the flesh.

Brevity Brevity is the soul of wit.

Brew As you brew, so shall you bake.

Bribe A bribe will enter without knocking.

Brimmer There is no deceit in a brimmer.

Broken Leg A broken leg is not healed by a silk stocking.

Burden A burden which one chooses is not felt.

Burden The back is made for the burden.

Burden No one knows the weight of another's burden.

Burdens The greatest burdens are not the gainfullest.

Burnt Child A burnt child dreads the fire.

Business Business is the salt of life.

Business Every man as his business lies.

Bush A bad bush is better than the open field.

Busy Who more busy than they that have least to do.

Butcher Better pay the butcher than the doctor.

Butter Butter is gold in the morning, silver at noon, lead at night.

Butter Why, butter would not melt in his mouth!

Butter What is a pound of butter amongst a kennel of hounds?

Butter Once a year butter is in the cow's horn.

Buttered He knows on which side his bread is buttered.

Buy Do not buy a pig in a poke.

Buyer Let the buyer look out for himself.

Buys Who buys hath need of a hundred eyes. Who sells hath need of one.

C

Cake You cannot eat your cake and have it.

Calm Sea In a calm sea every man is a pilot.

Calm Weather Calm weather in June sets corn in tune.

Can A man can do more than he can.

Candle Burn not your candle at both ends at once.

Candlemas On Candlemas day you must have half your straw and half your hay.

Candlemas If Candlemas day be fair and bright, Winter will have another flight; If on Candlemas day it be shower and rain, Winter is gone, and will not come again.

Candlemas When Candlemas day is come and gone, The snow lies on a hot stone.

Candlemas Day The hind had as lief see his wife on the bier, As Candlemas day should be pleasant and clear.

Candlemas Day On Candlemas day throw candle and candle-stick away.

Cap If the cap fit, wear it.

Captain Be captain of your own ship.

Carcase Where the carcase is, there will the eagles be gathered together.

Cards Many can pack the cards that cannot play.

Care Care's no cure.

Care Care will kill a cat.

Care Take care of the pence, and the pounds will take care of themselves.

Care not "Care not," would have.

Carry Don't run away with more than you can carry.

Carrying Coals Like carrying coals to Newcastle.

Castles Tis easy to build castles in the air.

Cash Rolling in cash he can't use, like a cat in a corn-bin.

Castle An Englishman's house is his castle.

Cat When the cat's away, The mice will play.

Cat A cat may look at a king.

Cat The cat is hungry when a crust contents her.

Cat The cat sees not the mouse ever.

Cats I'll keep no more cats than will catch mice.

Cat A cat has nine lives, yet care will kill a cat.

Cat When the cat winketh, little wots the mouse what the cat thinketh.

Cat Though the cat winks awhile, yet sure she is not blind.

Cat A cat loves fish, but she's loth to wet her feet.

Catch Catch that catch may.

Cause It's a bad cause that none dare speak in.

Caution Those are wise who learn caution from their own experience; but those are wiser who learn it from the experience of others.

Certain There is nothing certain in this life but death and taxes!

Certainty Never quit certainty for hope.

Chaff I'm too old a bird to be caught by chaff.

Chalk As like as chalk and cheese.

Chamber The chamber of sickness is the chapel of devotion.

Chance Look to the main chance.

Chance He that leaves certainty and sticks to chance, When fools pipe he may dance.

Chanceth It chanceth in an hour that comes not in seven years.

Change Change of pasture makes fat calves.

Charitable The charitable give out at the door, and God puts in at the window.

Charity Charity begins at home.

Chastiseth He that chastiseth one, amendeth many.

Cheese Cheese it is a peevish elf, It digests all things but itself.

Cheese After cheese comes nothing.

Cheese If you would have a good cheese, and have'n old, You must turn'n seven times before he is cold.

Cherry A cherry year, a merry year.

Chickens Count not your chickens before they are hatched.

Chiding Woe to the house where there is no chiding.

Child Train up a child in the way he should go, and when he is old he will not depart from it.

Child A child may have too much of his mother's blessing.

Child's Pig Child's pig, but father's bacon.

Children Children and fools speak the truth.

Children Children and fools have merry lives.

Children Children and chickens must be always picking.

Children Children are poor men's riches.

Children Children should hear, see, and say nothing.

Children When children stand quiet they have done some harm.

Children Children are certain cares, but very uncertain comforts.

Children Children suck the mother when they are young, and the father when they are old.

Chink So we have the chink, we'll bear the stink.

Chip A chip of the old block.

Christmas Christmas comes but once a year.

Christmas Green Christmas, white Easter.

Christmas They talk of Christmas so long that it comes.

Christmas Day If Christmas Day on a Monday be, A great winter that year you will see.

Church Where God hath His church the devil will have his chapel.

Churches Pater-noster built churches, and Our Father pulls them down.

Civil Words Civil words cost nothing, and go a long way.

Claw Claw me, and I will claw you.

Clear As clear as mud.

Clerk 'Tis the clerk makes the justice.

Climb Climb not too high, lest the fall be the greater.

Climbed Who never climbed, never fell.

Climbers Hasty climbers have sudden falls.

Cloak Have not the cloak to make when it begins to rain.

Cloak Though the sun shines, leave not your cloak at home.

Clock The clock goes as it pleases the clerk.

Close Mouth A close mouth catcheth no flies.

Clothes It is good keeping his clothes who is going to swim.

Cloud Every cloud hath a silver lining.

Clouds Clouds that the sun builds up darken him.

Clouds When the clouds are on the hills, They'll come down by the mills.

Clouds After clouds comes clear weather.

Cloudy Cloudy mornings turn to clear evenings.

Clover He is in clover.

Clown   Even a clown clings to his cloak when it rains.

Coat   Cut your coat according to your cloth.

Coat   It's not the gay coat that makes the gentleman.

Cobble   They that can cobble and clout,Shall have work when others go without.

Cobbler   Let not the cobbler go beyond his last.

Cobbler's Wife   Who goes worse shod than the cobbler's wife?

Cock   If the cock moult before the hen,We shall have weather thick and thin;But if the hen moult before the cock,We shall have weather hard as a block.

Cock   The cock crows and the hen goes.

Cock   Every cock is proud on his own dunghill.

Coin   Where coin's not common, commons must be scant.

Coin   Much coin much care.

Cold April   A cold April a barn will fill.

Cold May   A cold May and a windyMakes a full barn and a findy.

Coldest Flint   In the coldest flint there is hot fire.

Colours   It's an ill battle where the devil carries the colours.

Colt   When you ride a young colt see your saddle be well girt.

Company   Two's company and three's none.

Company   Tell me what company you keep, and I will tell you who you are.

Company   It's good to have company in trouble.

Company   Company in distress,Makes trouble less.

Companion   A merry companion on the road is as good as a nag.

Companion   There's no companion like a penny.

Comparisons   Comparisons are odious.

Complain They complain wrongfully of the sea, who twice suffer shipwreck.

Complexion Cold of complexion, good of condition.

Conceals A woman conceals what she knows not.

Confession A generous confession disarms slander.

Confession Confession of a fault makes half amends for it.

Confession Open confession is good for the soul.

Conquest It is no small conquest to overcome yourself.

Conscience A clear conscience is a sure card.

Constant Dropping Constant dropping wears the stone.

Consumed When all is consumed repentance comes too late.

Content Content is the true philosopher's stone.

Contented A contented mind is a continual feast.

Contented He that hath nothing is not contented.

Contented He may well be contented who needs neither borrow nor flatter.

Contented People are sometimes better contented full than fasting.

Contentment The greatest wealth is contentment with a little.

Corn Look at your corn in May, You'll come weeping away;- Look at the same in June You'll come home in another tune.

Corn Corn is cleansed with the wind, and the soul with chastening.

Cottage I'll not change a cottage in possession for a kingdom in reversion.

Counsel Counsel is never out of date.

Counsels Counsels in wine seldom prosper.

Counsel In wiving and thriving men should take counsel of all the world.

Counsel Three may keep counsel, if two be away.

Counselled He that will not be counselled cannot be helped.

Count Count not your chickens before they be hatched.

Country In every country the sun riseth in the morning.

Country You must go into the country to hear what news at London.

Couple Every couple is not a pair.

Court A friend at court is better than a penny in the purse.

Court Far from court, far from care.

Courts Courts have no almanacks.

Courtesy Less of your courtesy, and more of your purse.

Courtesy Courtesy on one side never lasts long.

Courtship Men dream in courtship but in wedlock wake.

Cousin Call me cousin; but cozen me not.

Coverlet Stretch your legs according to your coverlet.

Covers He covers me with his wings, and bites me with his bill.

Covet Covet nothing over much.

Covetousness Covetousness brings nothing home.

Cow Many a good cow hath had a bad calf.

Cow Look to the cow, and the sow, and the wheat mow, and all will be well enow.

Cowards Cowards are always cruel.

Cowardice Cowardice is afraid to be known or seen.

Crabs The greatest crabs are not always the best meat.

Crack He must crack the nut that would eat the kernel.

Craft Craft bringeth nothing home.

Crafts Of all crafts, to be an honest man is the master-craft.

Crafty Crafty evasions save not the truth.

Crazy Ship To a crazy ship all winds are contrary.

Creaking Gate A creaking gate hangs longest on its hinges.

Creaks The worst wheel of a cart creaks most.

Credit Credit lost is a Venice glass broken.

Creditors Creditors have better memories than debtors.

Creep First creep and then go.

Critics Critics are like brushers of other men's clothes.

Crooked A crooked tree will have a crooked shadow.

Crooked Crooked logs make straight fires.

Cross No cross, no crown.

Cross Every cross has its inscription.

Crosses Crosses are ladders for getting to heaven.

Crosses Crosses are ladders that lead to heaven.

Crow The crow thinks her own bird fairest.

Crow A crow is never the whiter for washing herself often.

Crows It never goes well when the hen crows.

Cruelty Cruelty is a tyrant always attended by fear.

Cruelty Cruelty is a devil's delight.

Crumbs Where are the crumbs there are the chickens.

Cry Don't cry out before you're hurt.

Cry Great cry and little wool.

Cuckoo When the cuckoo comes to the bare thorn, Sell your cow and buy your corn, But when she comes to a full bit, Sell your corn, and buy your sheep.

Cured What cannot be cured must be endured.

Curses Curses are like chickens, they come home to roost.

Custom Custom is second nature.

Custom Once a use and ever a custom.

Custom   Custom makes anything easy.

Custom (bad)   A bad custom is like a good cake, better broken than kept.

Cut   Cut and come again.

Cut   No cut like unkindness.

Cut   I had not cut my wise teeth.

Cuts   Desperate cuts must have desperate cures.

D

Dance   No longer pipe, no longer dance.

Dances   He dances well to whom fortune pipes.

Dancing   They love dancing well that dance among thorns.

Danger   The danger's past, and God's forgotten.

Dainty Dogs   Dainty dogs may have to eat dirty puddings.

Dark   It is as good to be in the dark as without light.

Dark Man   A dark man's a jewel in a fair woman's eye.

Dark   He that gropes in the dark finds that he would not.

Daughter   My son is my son till he marries a wife, But my daughter's my daughter all the days of her life.

Daughter   He that would the daughter win, Must with the mother first begin.

Daylight   Daylight will peep through a small hole.

Dead   As dead as a door-nail.

Dead Man's Shoes   He that waits for a dead man's shoes may go long enough barefoot.

Deaf   There are none so deaf as those who will not hear.

Deaf Man   Tell that tale to a deaf man.

Dearth   It's a wicked thing to make a dearth one's garner.

Death   Death keeps no calendar.

Death   Death is deaf and hears no denial.

Death   Nothing is surer than death.

Death   After death the doctor.

Debt   Debt is the worst kind of poverty.

Debt   Out of debt, out of danger.

Deepest Water   In the deepest water is the best fishing.

Deeds   Deeds are fruits, words are but leaves.

Deeds   A life spent worthily should be measured by deeds—not years.

Delays   Delays are dangerous.

Depth   Never venture out of your depth until you can swim.

Desert   Desert and reward seldom keep company.

Deserve   First deserve and then desire.

Desires   Desires are nourished by delays.

Despises   What one man despises, another craves.

Destiny   Hanging and wiving go by destiny.

Devil   Talk of the devil and he'll be sure to appear.

Devil   He that hath shipped the devil must make the best of him.

Devil   Give the devil his due.

Devil   Make not the devil blacker than he is.

Devil   He needs must go that the devil drives.

Devil   One must sometimes hold a candle to the devil.

Devil   The devil is not always at one door.

Devil   The Devil Was Sick, the Devil a Monk Would Be; The Devil Grew Well, the Devil a Monk Was He.

Dew St   Bartholomew brings the cold dew.

Die   Never say die.

Die   Young men may die, old men must.

Diligence   Diligence is a good patrimony.

Diligence   Diligence is the mother of good fortune.

Dinner   After dinner sit awhile, after supper walk a mile.

Dinner   He who would enjoy his friend's dinner should not look into the kitchen.

Distress   Two in distress make sorrows less.

Discourse   Sweet discourse makes short days and nights.

Discreet   Discreet women have neither eyes nor ears.

Discretion   An ounce of discretion is worth a pound of wit.

Disease   Disease is oft the tax of pleasure.

Disease   To know the disease is half the cure.

Dish   The first dish pleaseth all.

Do   Do as you would be done by.

Do   We must do as we may, if we cannot do as we would.

Dock   In dock, out nettle.

Doctor   A doctor and a clown know more than a doctor alone.

Doctor   An old doctor, a young lawyer.

Dog   Every dog has his day.

Dog   A good dog deserves a good bone.

Dog   It's a bad dog that deserves not a crust.

Dogs Bark   Dogs bark before they bite.

Done   If you wish a thing done, go; if not, send.

Doomsday   A thousand pounds and a pottle of hay is all one thing at doomsday.

Door   When one door shuts another opens.

Do Well   Do well, and have well.

Down   He that's down, down with him.

Draw   You may draw him which way you will, with a twine thread.

Drowning Man   A drowning man will catch at a straw.

Drink   Drink water like an ox, wine like a king of Spain.

Drink   He who drinks when he is not dry, will be dry when he has no drink.

Drive   Drive not a second nail till the first is clenched.

Drops   Many drops make a shower.

Drought   If the ash before the oak comes out, There has been, or there will be drought.

Drowned   Pour not water on a drowned mouse.

Drunk   Ever drunk, ever dry.

Drunken   A drunken night makes a cloudy morning.

Drunken Folk   Drunken folk often speak truth.

Drunkenness   What soberness conceals, drunkenness reveals.

Dry Bread   Dry bread at home is better than roast beef abroad.

Dry Cough   A dry cough is the trumpeter of death.

Dry May   A dry May and a dripping June,Does surely bring all things in tune.

E

Early Early to bed, and early to rise, Makes a man healthy, wealthy, and wise.

Early Early sow, early mow.

Early Bird 'Tis the early bird catches the worm.

Ears Little pitchers have long ears.

Ears Walls have ears.

Ears Wider ears and a shorter tongue.

Ease A pennyworth of ease is worth a penny.

Ease Think of ease, but work on.

Easily Done That which is easily done is soon believed.

Eat Live not to eat, but eat to live.

Eat Eat a bit before you drink.

Eat Eat at pleasure, Drink by measure.

Eating Eating and drinking takes away one's appetite.

Edged Tools It is ill meddling with edged tools.

Eel You cannot hide an eel in a sack.

Eggs Don't put all your eggs into one basket.

Egg-Shell 'Tis hard to sail o'er the sea in an egg-shell.

Elbow Rub your sore eye with your elbow.

Elbow Grease Give it plenty of elbow grease.

Empty House Better an empty house than a bad tenant.

Empty Purse An empty purse fills the face with wrinkles.

Empty Purse That's but an empty purse that's full of other men's money.

Empty Vessels Empty vessels make the greatest sound.

End Everything hath an end, and a pudding hath two.

Endureth He that endureth is not overcome.

England England is the Paradise of women.

Englishman An Englishman's house is his castle.

Enough Enough is as good as a feast.

Enough Enough and to spare is too much.

Enough There's never enough where nothing's left.

Envied Better be envied than pitied.

Envy Envy never enriched any man.

Epitaph He lies like an epitaph.

Err To err is human; to forgive divine.

Errand Send a wise man on an errand and say nothing to him.

Escapes 'Tis a hard battle where none escapes.

Estate He that throws away his estate with his hands, goes afterwards to pick it upon his feet.

Esteems He that knows himself best, esteems himself least.

Evening An evening red and a morning grey, Is a sign of a fair day.

Everybody He had need rise betimes that would please everybody.

Everybody's Business Everybody's business is nobody's business.

Every Man Every man for himself, and God for us all.

Every Tub Let every tub stand on its own bottom.

Evil Evil communications corrupt good manners.

Evil If you must have an evil, choose a little one.

Evil That which is evil is soon learnt.

Evil Evil is wrought by want of thought, As well as want of heart.

Evil name   The evil wound is cured, but not the evil name.

Evil Gotten   Evil gotten, evil spent.

Evil Grain   Of evil grain no good seed can come.

Evils   Of two evils choose the lesser.

Example   Example teaches more than precept.

Exchange   Exchange is no robbery.

Excuse   A bad excuse is better than none at all.

Expenses   Proportion your expenses to what you have, not to what you expect.

Experience   Experience is a dear school, but it is the only one we are apt to learn in.

Experience   Experience is the mistress of fools.

Extremes   Extremes seldom last long.

Extremes   Extremes meet.

Eye   Better one eye than quite blind.

Eye   What the eye sees not, the heart rues not.

Eye   You should never touch your eye but with your elbow.

Eye   What the eye does not see the heart does not grieve for.

Eye-Witness   One eye-witness is better than ten hearsays.

F

Face Her face was her fortune.

Fact A single fact is worth a ship-load of argument.

Faint Heart Faint heart never won a fair lady.

Faint Praise Faint praise is disparagement.

Fair and Foolish Fair and foolish, black and proud, Long and lazy, little and loud.

Fair and Softly Fair and softly go far in a day.

Fair Faces Fair faces need no paint.

Fair Face A fair face may hide a foul heart.

Fair Feathers Fair feathers make fair fowls.

Faith Love asks faith, and faith asks firmness.

Fall One may sooner fall than rise.

Fall If a man once fall, all will tread on him.

Falls When the tree falls every man runs with his hatchet.

Falling Keeping from falling is better than helping up.

False Report A false report rides post.

Familiarity Familiarity breeds contempt.

Famine After a famine in the stall, Comes a famine in the hall.

Famine Under water famine, under snow bread.

Famine A famine in England begins at the horse-manger.

Fancy Fancy passes beauty.

Fancy Fancy goes a long way.

Fancy Fancy may bolt bran and think it flour.

Fare Worse You may go farther and fare worse.

Fashion As good to be out of the world as out of the fashion.

Fast Bind Fast bind, fast find.

Fat Hog Every one basteth the fat hog, while the lean one burneth.

Fault Every one puts his fault on the times.

Fault A fault once denied is twice committed.

Fault-Finders Fault-finders should be fault-menders.

Faults Every one's faults are not written on their foreheads.

Faults Every man hath his faults.

Faults God send me a friend that may tell me my faults; if not, an enemy, he will be sure to.

Faulty The faulty stands on his guard.

Feast A feast is not made of mushrooms only.

Feast-Making Merry is the feast-making until we come to the reckoning.

Feasts Fools make feasts, and wise men eat them.

Feathers Fine feathers make fine birds.

Feather Feather by feather the goose is plucked.

February February makes a bridge, and March breaks it.

February February fill dike, be it black or be it white; But if it be white, it's the better to like.

Feed Sparingly Feed sparingly, and defy the physician.

Feet Stretch not your feetBeyond the sheet.

Fellowship Love and lordship like no fellowship.

Fetters No man loves his fetters, though of gold.

Few Friends Have but few friends, though many acquaintances.

Few Words Where hearts are trueFew words will do.

Fiddler The fifer don't pay a fiddler.

Fiddler Let not the fiddler play the fife, Nor fifer play the fiddle.

Fiddler's Fare Fiddler's fare; meat, drink, and money.

Fields Fields have eyes, and woods have ears.

Finger He wants to have a finger in every pie.

First Blow The first blow is half the battle.

First Come First come, first served.

Fire and Water Fire and water are good servants but bad masters.

Fire Well may he smell of fire whose gown burneth.

Fish He that would catch fish must not mind getting wet.

Fish 'Tis good fish if it were but caught.

Fish The best fish are near the bottom.

Fish I have other fish to fry.

Fish Make not fish of one, and flesh of another.

Fish Fish are not to be caught by a birdcall.

Fish (good) There's as good fish in the sea as were ever caught.

Fishes' Mouth When the wind's in the south, It blows the bait into the fishes' mouth.

Fisheth On He fisheth on that catcheth one.

Fishing It's good fishing in troubled waters.

Fits Every shoe fits not every foot.

Five He's up at five, And he will thrive.

Flax Get thy spindle and thy distaff ready, and God will send thee flax.

Flay No man can flay a stone.

Fleeceth Where every hand fleeceth, the sheep go naked.

Flood A May flood never did good.

Flowers Flowers are the pledge of fruit.

Flourish It is one thing to flourish and another to fight.

Flying No flying without wings.

Follies Happy is he who knows his follies in his youth.

Fool No one is a fool always; every one sometimes.

Fool A fool may ask more questions in half an hour than a wise man can answer in seven years.

Fool A fool may give a wise man counsel.

Fool One fool makes many.

Fool Every man is either a fool or a physician after thirty years of age.

Fool (old) An old fool is the worst of fools.

Fool Better it is to meet a bear bereaved of her whelps, than a fool in his folly.

Fool A fool is fulsome.

Fool Thinks As the fool thinks, so the bell chinks.

Fools Fools set stools for wise folk to stumble at.

Fool's Bolt A fool's bolt is soon shot.

Fools Build Fools build houses, and wise men buy them.

Forbearance Forbearance is no acquittance.

Forbidden Fruit Forbidden fruit is sweet.

Forced Fruits Forced fruits fail in flavour.

Forecast Forecast is better than work hard.

Forego Forego, forget, forgive, Then happy you shall live.

Foremost Dog The foremost dog catches the hare.

Forewarned Forewarned is forearmed.

Forget To forget a wrong is the best revenge.

Forgive Forgive and forget.

Forgotten Eaten bread is soon forgotten.

Fortune   Fortune favours the brave.

Fortune   Every man is the architect of his fortune.

Fortune   Change of fortune is the lot of life.

Fortune   Better a fortune in her than on her.

Fortune   When fortune smiles take the advantage.

Fortune   Knocks   Fortune knocks once at least at every man's gate.

Foul Hands   Foul hands befoul all they touch.

Four Farthings   Four farthings and a thimble make a tailor's pocket jingle.

Fox   The fox knows much, but more he that catcheth him.

Fox   A fox should not be of the jury at a goose trial.

Fox   When the fox preaches, beware of your geese.

Foxes   Foxes, when they cannot reach the grapes, say they are not ripe.

Fox Runs   Though the fox runs the chicken hath wings.

Fret   Two things you won't fret o'er, If you're a wise man—The thing you can't help, And the thing that you can.

Friday   He that sings on Friday shall weep on Sunday.

Friday   As the Friday, so the Sunday, As the Sunday, so the week.

Friday's Sail   Friday's sail, sure to fail.

Friend   A friend is not so soon gotten as lost.

Friend   A friend in need is a friend indeed.

Friend   He loseth nothing who keeps God for his friend.

Friend   Make not thy friend too cheap to thee, nor thyself to thy friend.

Friend   In time of prosperity friends will be plenty, In time of adversity, not one among twenty.

Friends   Save me from my friends.

Friends All are not friends that speak us fair.

Friendship Love and lordship never like friendship.

Frost What God will, no frost can kill.

Frosts So many frosts in March, so many in May.

Fruit If you would fruit have, You must bring the leaf to the grave.

Fruit Such as the tree is, such is the fruit.

Fruit If you would enjoy the fruit, pluck not the flower.

Frugality Frugality makes an easy chair for old age.

Frugality Frugality is an estate.

Frying-Pan Out of the frying-pan into the fire.

Fuel Take away fuel, take away flame.

Full Purse A full purse makes the mouth to speak.

Full Purse A full purse never lacketh friends.

G

Gains No gains without pains.

Galled Horse Touch a galled horse, and he will wince.

Gapeth He that gapeth until he be fedWell may he gape until he be dead.

Garden Many things grow in the garden that were never planted there.

Gardening This rule in gardening never forget,To sow dry and set wet.

Garland One flower makes no garland.

Gems Gems must not be valued by what they are set in.

Gentility Gentility without ability is worse than plain beggary.

Gentle Strokes Gentle strokes make the sweetest harmony.

Get Get what you can, and what you get, hold,'Tis the stone which will turn your lead into gold.

Gift Horse Look not a gift horse in the mouth.

Gift A gift with a kind countenance is a double gift.

Give To give and keep there is need of wit.

Giveth He giveth twice who gives in a trice.

Giving Giving to the poorIncreaseth your store.

Gladness A man of gladness seldom falls into madness.

Glass What your glass tells you will not be told by counsel.

Glass Who loves his glass without a G,Take away L and that is he.

Glass Houses Those who live in glass houses should not throw stones.

Glasses The more women look in their glasses, the less they look to their houses.

Glitters All that glitters is not gold.

Gnats Men strain at gnats, and swallow camels!

Go If you want a thing done, go; if not, send.

Go About Better go about than fall into the ditch.

God God sends meat, and the devil sends cooks.

God One God, no more; but friends good store.

Godfathers When the child is christened, you may have godfathers enough.

God wills When God wills, all winds bring rain.

Gold A man may buy gold too dear.

Gold Gold alone makes not prosperity.

Gold As good as gold.

Gold Gold goes in at any gate, except Heaven's.

Gold No lock will hold 'Gainst the power of gold.

Golden We must not look for a golden life in an iron age.

Gold Dust Gold dust blinds all eyes.

Good Do all the good you talk of; but talk not of all the good you do.

Good Good and quickly seldom meet.

Good No man knows better what good is than he that has an endured evil.

Good Though good be good yet better carries it.

Good Cheer When good cheer is lacking our friends will be packing.

Good Word A good word is as soon said as an ill one.

Good Counsel Good counsel never comes too late.

Good Friend He's a good friend that speaks well of us behind our backs.

Good Harvests Good harvests make men prodigal, bad ones provident.

Good Maxim A good maxim is never out of season.

Good Money It is no use throwing good money after bad.

Good Name The wife that cxpccts to havc a good namcIs always at home as if she were lame, And the maid that is honest her chiefest delightIs still to be doing from morning to night.

Goods A man may lose his goods for want of demanding them.

Good Things God reacheth us good things with our own hands.

Good Thing One can never have too much of a good thing.

Good Turns One never loseth by doing good turns.

Good Turn One good turn deserves another.

Good Words Good words without deedsAre rushes and reeds.

Gown The gown is hers who wears it, and the world is his who enjoys it.

Grasp Grasp no more than thy hand will hold.

Grain Never split timber against the grain.

Grasp Grasp all, lose all.

Grass March grass never did good.

Grass If the grass grow in Janiveer,It grows the worse for't all the year.

Grass While the grass grows the steed starves.

Grass Grass grows not upon the highway.

Graves We shall lie all alike in our graves.

Great Dowry A great dowry is a bed full of troubles.

Great Marks Great marks are soonest hit.

Great Ones There would be no great ones if there were no little.

Great Ship A great ship needs deep waters.

Green Wood Green wood makes a hot fire.

Green Wound A green wound is soon healed.

Green Winter A green winter makes a fat churchyard.

Grey Hairs Gray hairs are death's blossoms.

Grief Grief pent up will burst the heart.

Grind The mill cannot grind with the water that is past.

Guest An unbidden guest must bring his own stool with him.

Guest 'Tis an ill guest that never drinks to his host.

Guilty Conscience A guilty conscience needs no accuser.

H

Hail   Hail brings frost in the tail.

Half a Loaf   Half a loaf is better than no bread.

Half Hanged   Better be half hanged than ill wed.

Hand-Saw   A hand-saw is a good thing, but not to shave with.

Hand-Saw   He knows not a hawk from a hand-saw.

Handsome   He who is not handsome at twenty, nor strong at thirty, nor wise at forty, nor rich at fifty, will never be handsome, strong, rich, or wise.

Hanged   He who is born to be hanged will never be drowned.

Hanged   One may as well be hanged for a sheep as a lamb.

Hanging   There are many ways of killing a dog beside hanging him.

Happy   Happy is the bride the sun shines on, And the corpse the rain rains on.

Hare   Where we least think, there goeth the hare away.

Hardly Ever   "Hardly ever" saves many a lie.

Hare   Little dogs start the hare, but great ones catch it.

Hare Skin   Sell not the hare's skin before you have caught him.

Harm   Harm watch, harm catch.

Harms   Wise men learn by others' harms, fools by their own.

Harvest   He that hath a good harvest may be content with some thistles.

Haste   More haste worse speed.

Haste   Haste trips up its own heels.

Haste   Over haste makes certain waste.

Haste   Haste over nothing but catching fleas.

Hasty Men   Hasty men never lack woe.

Hasty Resolutions   Hasty resolutions seldom speed well.

Hat   Pull down your hat on the wind side.

Hatchet   When the tree is down, every one runs with his hatchet.

Haven   'Tis safe riding in a good haven.

Hay   Make hay while the sun shines.

Head   Man is the head, but woman turns it.

Head   He that hath no head, needs no hat.

Head   Better be the head of an ass than the tail of a horse.

Headache   When the head aches, all the body is the worse.

Healed   A man is not so soon healed as hurt.

Healeth   God healeth, and the physician hath the thanks.

Health   Health is better than wealth.

Heart   What the heart thinketh, the tongue speaketh.

Hearts   Hearts may agree though heads differ.

Hedge   Where the hedge is lowest, men commonly leap over.

Hedge   A low hedge is easily leapt over.

Hedge   A hedge betweenKeeps friendship green.

Hedges   Hedges have eyes, and walls have ears.

Heed   Good take heed doth surely speed.

Heels   One pair of heels is often worth two pair of hands.

Hen Crows   It is a sad house where the hen crows louder than the cock.

Hid   Love and a cough cannot be hid.

Hide   You cannot hide an eel in a sack.

Hide Hide nothing from thy minister, physician, and lawyer.

High Places High places have their precipices.

High Winds High winds blow on high hills.

Himself Every man is best known to himself.

Himself He is not wise that is not wise for himself.

Hind To fright a hind is not the way to catch her.

Hindermost Dog The hindermost dog may catch the hare.

Hobby Happy is the man that has a hobby.

Hobby-Horse Every man has his hobby-horse.

Hog A hog in armour is still but a hog.

Holloa Do not holloa till you are out of the wood.

Home Home is home, be it ever so homely.

Honesty Honesty is the best policy; but he who acts on this principle is not an honest man.

Honesty A man never surfeits of too much honesty.

Honour Better poor with honour than rich with shame.

Honour Honour and ease are seldom bed-fellows.

Honour Where honour ceaseth, there knowledge decreaseth.

Hoop He giveth one knock on the hoop, and another on the barrel.

Hope Hope deferred maketh the heart sick.

Hope Hope humbles more than despair.

Hope Hope is a good breakfast, but a bad supper.

Hope If it were not for hope, the heart would break.

Hops Till St. James's day be come and gone, You may have hops, or you may have none.

Horn All are not hunters that blow the horn.

Horse A good horse cannot be of a bad colour.

Horse A good horse often wants a good spur.

Horse 'Tis an ill horse will not carry his own provender.

Horse One man may lead a horse to water, but fifty cannot make him drink.

Hot Love Hot love is soon cold.

Hot May A hot May makes a fat churchyard.

Hounds Hold not with the hounds and run with the hare.

House He that buys a house ready wrought, Hath many a pin and nail for nought.

House Better one's house too little one day, than too big all the year round.

Householders Wishers and woulders are never good house-holders.

Housekeeper A noble house-keeper needs no doors.

Humour Every man has his humour.

Humours The stillest humours are always the worst.

Hundred Years It is all one a hundred years hence.

Hung As well be hung for a sheep as a lamb.

Hunger Hunger costs little; daintiness much.

Hunger Hunger will break through stone walls.

Hunger Hunger makes short devotion.

Hunger Hunger makes hard bones sweet beans.

Hunger Hunger is the finest sauce.

Hungry Flies Hungry flies bite sore.

Hungry Horse A hungry horse makes a clean manger.

Hungry Man A hungry man, an angry man.

Hungry Men Hungry men think the cook lazy.

Hungry Men Bitter is sweet to hungry men.

Husband   Be a good husband, and you will get a penny to spend, a penny to lend, and a penny for a friend.

Husband   In the husband wisdom, in the wife gentleness.

I

Idle B rain   An idle brain is the devil's workshop.

Idle Folk   Idle folk have the least leisure.

Idle Folk   Idle folk take the most pains.

Idle   A young man idle, an old man needy.

Idle   Better be idle than ill employed.

Idleness   Idleness is the key of beggary.

Idleness   Of idleness comes no goodness.

Idleness   Idleness is the root of all evil.

Idleness   Idleness must thank itself if it goes barefoot.

Ignorant   The ignorant think all things wrong which they cannot understand.

Ill Bird   It is an ill bird that defiles its own nest.

Ill Dog   'Tis an ill dog that deserves not a bone.

Ill Fortune   He who hath no ill fortune, is dazed with good.

Ill Got   Ill got, ill spent.

Ill Gotten   Ill gotten gains seldom prosper.

Ill Luck   When ill luck falls asleep, let nobody wake her.

Ill News   Ill news comes apace.

Ill Weeds   Ill weeds grow apace.

Ill Word   One ill word asketh another.

Impossible   Nothing is impossible to a willing mind.

Impudence   Impudence is not courage.

Inch Give him an inch, and he'll take an ell.

Inches God never measures men by inches.

Industry Industry is fortune's right hand and frugality her left.

Infirmities Jest not at another's infirmities.

Ingratitude Ingratitude is the daughter of pride.

Injury Pocket an injury.

Inn He goes not out of his way that goes to a good inn.

Instinct Woman's instinct is often truer than man's reasoning.

Intentions Hell is paved with good intentions.

Irons He that hath many irons in the fire, some of them will cool.

Itch Itch and ease can no man please.

J

Jack Jack-in-office is a great man.

Jack Every Jack has his Jill.

Janiveer If Janiveer calends be summerly gay' Twill be winterly weather till calends of May.

Janiveer Who in Janiveer sows oats, gets gold and groats.

Jest Better lose a jest than a friend.

Jest Many a true word is spoken in jest.

Jesting Jesting lies bring serious sorrows.

Jests Jests, like sweetmeats, are often sour sauce.

Journey 'Tis a great journey to the world's end.

Joy No joy without annoy.

Joy There's no joy without alloy.

Joy Joy surfeited turns to sorrow.

Judge Judge not of men or things at first sight.

Judge Judge not a ship as she lies on the stocks.

Judgment He hath a good judgment who is apt to distrust his own.

June Calm weather in June-Sets corn in tune.

July If the first of July, it be rainy weather,'Twill rain more or less for four weeks together.

Just Just is honest, and honest is just.

K

Keep Keep a thing seven years, and you will find a use for it.

Keep Keep some till more come.

Kernel He that will eat the kernel, must crack the nut.

Key The wife is the key of the house.

Keys All the keys hang not at one man's girdle.

Kin Still stand by kinThrough thick and thin.

Kindled Wood half burnt is easily kindled.

Kindness Kindness will always conquer.

Kindnesses Kindnesses, like grain, increase by sowing.

Kinsfolk Many kinsfolk, few friends.

Kiss As easy kiss my hand.

Kiss Many kiss the child for the nurse's sake.

Kissing Kissing goes by favour.

Kitchen A fat kitchen, a lean will.

Kitchen The taste of the kitchen is better than the smell.

Kitchen Silks and satins put out the fire in the kitchen.

Knavery Knavery may serve for a turn, but honesty is best in the long run.

Knaves Knaves and fools divide the world.

Knaves When knaves fall out, true men come by their goods.

Knot He tied a knot with his tongue he couldn't undo with his teeth.

Knots   Fools tie knots and wise men loose them.

Knotty Timber   To split knotty timber use smooth wedges.

Knowledge   Knowledge is power.

Knowledge   Knowledge in youth is wisdom in age.

Knowledge   The knowledge of the disease is half the cure.

Knowledge   Knowledge, like physic, is more plague than profit, if it arrives too late.

Knowledge   An ounce of knowledge may be worth a pound of comfort.

L

Labours He that labours and thrives, spins gold.

Labour Labour warms, sloth harms.

Ladle The ladle cools the pot.

Ladder Step after step the ladder is ascended.

Lamb's Tail A woman's tongue wags like a lamb's tail.

Lame The lame goeth as far as the staggerer.

Lammas After Lammas corn ripens as much by night as by day.

Land Land was never lost for want of an heir.

Land Many a one for land, Takes a fool by the hand.

Lantern On a dark night an owl would be glad of a lantern.

Last Straw It is the last straw that breaks the camel's back.

Late Better late than never.

Laugh Let them laugh that win.

Laugh That's where the laugh comes in.

Laugh They laugh the loudest who have least to lose.

Law In a thousand pounds of law there's not an ounce of love.

Law The law is not the same at morning and night.

Law He that loves law will get his fill.

Law Makers Law makers should not be law breakers.

Laws Laws catch flies, but let hornets go free.

Laws Laws, like spiders' webs, are wrought, Large flies break through, the small are caught.

Laws Laws were made for rogues.

Lawyer A good lawyer, an evil neighbour.

Lawyers Fair and softly as lawyers go to heaven.

Lazy Folk Lazy folk take the most pains.

Lead A man may lead a horse to the water, but he cannot make him drink unless he will.

Lead 'Tis folly to dig for lead with a silver shovel.

Leak A small leak will sink a great ship.

Learn Never too old to learn.

Learning Learning makes a man fit company for himself.

Least Least said is soonest mended.

Least Boy The least boy always carries the greatest fiddle.

Leather Nothing like leather.

Leech The empty leech sucks sore.

Lend He that doth not lend doth lose his friend.

Lend He would not lend his knife to the devil to stab himself.

Liar A liar should have a good memory.

Liars Liars have short wings.

Libel The greater truth, the greater libel.

Liberal The liberal man deviseth liberal things.

Liberty Too much liberty spoils all.

Lie One lie makes many.

Lies He lies as fast as a dog can trot.

Life Life is full of hazards, which experience neither bought nor taught will always enable us to foresee.

Life Life is half spent before we know what it is.

Life Life is sweet.

Life Life lies not in living, but in liking.

Life While there's life there's hope.

Light   He stands in his own light.

Light   Every light has its shadow.

Light   Every light is not the sun.

Light Gains   Light gains make a heavy purse.

Like   As like as two peas.

Like   Every one as they like best, as the good man said when he kissed his cow.

Like   Like father like son.

Like   Like will to like.

Lion   The lion's not half so fierce as he's painted.

Lips   Lips however rosy must be fed.

Listeners   Listeners never hear good of themselves.

Little   Little and often fills the purse.

Little   Little mother, little daughter.

Little Birds   Little birds may peck a dead lion.

Little Boats   Little boats must keep the shore.

Little Bodies   Little bodies have large souls.

Little Good   A little good is soon spent.

Little Goods   Little goods, little care.

Little Hole   One may see day at a little hole.

Little House   A little house well fill'd, A little land well till'd, And a little wife well will'd.

Little Minds   Little minds, like weak liquors, are soon soured.

Little Things   Little things please little minds.

Live   Everything would live.

Live   It's not how long, but how well, we live.

Live   Live and learn.

Live   Live and let live.

Liver (longest)   The longest liver dies at last.

Lives   He that lives not well one year sorrows for it seven.

Liveth He liveth long that liveth well.

Living Dog A living dog is better than a dead lion.

Load All lay load on the willing horse.

Lock You needn't lock the stable door when the steed is stolen.

Look Look before you leap.

Look They look one way and row another.

Looked for Long looked for comes at last.

Long Lane 'Tis a long lane that has no turning.

Longs He that longs most lacks most.

Longest Day The longest day must have an end.

Loquacity The loquacity of fools is a warning to the wise.

Lords New lords new laws.

Losers Losers are always in the wrong.

Loss He that goeth out with often loss, At last comes home by Weeping Cross.

Lost 'Tis not lost that comes at last.

Love Love is no lack.

Love Love is blind.

Love Love is the touchstone of virtue.

Love Love lives in cottages as well as in courts.

Love Love me little, love me long.

Love Love me, love my dog.

Love They love too much who die for love.

Love Whom we love best to them we can say least.

Love and a Cough Love and a cough cannot be hid.

Love (hot) Hot love is soon cold.

Lovers Lovers live on love, as larks on leeks.

Lowly Sit Lowly sit and be richly warm.

Luck Give a man luck, and throw him into the sea.

Luck The devil's children have the devil's luck.

Luck (ill) What is worse than ill-luck?

Lucky It is better to be born lucky than rich.

Lucky It's better to be lucky than wise.

Lucky Happy go lucky.

Lurch Never leave a friend in the lurch.

M

Maidens Maidens must be seen and not heard.

Malice Malice is mindful.

Malt Slow fire makes sweet malt.

Man A man at five may be a fool at fifteen.

Man Man proposes, God disposes.

Man Man doth what he can, and God what He will.

Manners Manners often make fortunes.

Many Hands Many hands make light work.

March March wind and May sun,Make clothes white and maids dun.

March March many weathers.

March Dust A bushel of March dust is worth a king's ransom.

Market A man must sell his ware at the rate of the market.

Market Forsake not the market for the toll.

Market If fools went not to market, bad ware would not be sold.

Market Three women and a goose make a market.

Marriage (ill) An ill marriage is a spring of ill fortune.

Marriage Marriage halves our griefs, and doubles our joys.

Marriages Marriages are made in heaven.

Marries He who marries for wealth sells his liberty.

Marry Marry in haste, repent at leisure.

Marry Bachelors, before you marry,Have a house wherein to tarry.

Marry If you regard old saws, mind, thus they say,'Tis bad to marry in the month of May.

Master Like master like man.

Master He that will too soon be his own master, will have a fool for his scholar.

Master No man is his craft's master the first day.

Master Marry above your match and you get a master.

Master One eye of the master sees more than four of the servants'.

Master-Craft Of all the crafts honesty is the master-craft.

Masters No man can serve two masters.

Master's Eye The master's eye makes the horse fat.

Master's Eye The master's eye does more work than his hands.

Matrimony Matrimony's a matter of money.

May be Every "may be" hath a "may not be."

May A windy March and a rainy April make a beautiful May.

May (cold) A cold May,Plenty of corn and hay.

Meadow A thin meadow is soon mowed.

Measure Good measure is a merry mean.

Measure With what measure ye mete it shall be measured to you again.

Measure Measure twice before you cut once.

Measures He measures your corn by his bushel.

Meat Much meat, much maladies.

Meat Meat is much, but manners is more.

Medium There's a medium between painting the face and not washing it.

Medlars Medlars are never good till they be rotten.

Medlars Time and straw make medlars ripe.

Mend It is never too late to mend.

Mend If every one would mend one, all would be mended.

Mend In the end things will mend.

Mercy Cry you mercy, who killed my cat?

Merry He that is of a merry heart hath a continual feast.

Merry It's good to be merry and wise.

Merry It is good to be merry at meat.

Merry Merry meet, merry part, merry meet again.

Merry As long lives a merry heart as a sad.

Merry Month The merry month of May.

Mettle Mettle is dangerous in a blind horse.

Milk Milk which will not be made into butter must be made into cheese.

Milk Who would keep a cow when he may have a bottle of milk for a penny!

Mill No mill, no meal.

Millstone I can see as far into a millstone as the picker.

Millstone The lower millstone grinds as well as the upper.

Mind Out of sight, out of mind.

Mind In the forehead and the eye, The picture of the mind doth lie.

Mind A woman's mind and winter wind often change.

Mind A wise man changes his mind; a fool never.

Mirth A pennyworth of mirth is worth a pound of sorrow.

Mischief A little mischief is too much.

Mischiefs Mischiefs come by the pound and go away by the ounce.

Misfortunes Misfortunes seldom come alone.

Miss A miss is as good as a mile.

Mists So many mists in March you see, So many frosts in May will be.

Misunderstanding Misunderstanding brings lies to town.

Mob The mob has many heads, but no brains.

Mocking Mocking is catching.

Modesty Modesty is the handmaid of virtue.

Monday Monday for wealth, Tuesday for health, Wednesday the best day of all; Thursday for crosses, Friday for losses, Saturday no luck at all.

Money Money is more easily made than made use of.

Money They who have money are troubled about it, And they who have none are troubled without it.

Money Money makes money.

Money Money often makes the man.

Money The abundance of money ruins youth.

Money A fool and his money are soon parted.

Money A fool may make money, but a wise man should spend it.

Money 'Tis money makes the mare to go.

Money He that hath no money needeth no purse.

Moon In the old of the moon, A cloudy morning bodes a fair afternoon.

Moon A Saturday's moonAlways comes too soon.

Moon The moon's not seen where the sun shines.

More The more the merrier; the fewer the better cheer.

Morning Lose an hour in the morning, and you'll be all day hunting for it.

Morning Sun The morning sun never lasts a day.

Most Do as most do, and fewest will speak ill of thee.

Most   Most take all.

Mother's Breath   The mother's breath is always sweet.

Mother's Heart   A mother's heart never grows old.

Mother-Wit   An ounce of mother-wit is worth a pound of clergy.

Mountain   Never make a mountain of a mole-hill.

Mountain   If the mountain will not go to Mahomet, let Mahomet go to the mountain.

Mouth Civility   Mouth civility costs little but is worth less.

Mouths   He that sends mouths sends meat.

Much   A fool demands much, but he's a greater that gives it.

Much   Much is expected where much is given.

Much   Much would have more, and lost all.

Muddles   Muddles at home make husbands roam.

Muffled Cats   Muffled cats are bad mousers.

Murder   Murder will out.

Music   Music helps not the toothache.

Music   Where music is no harm can be.

Musician   When a musician hath forgot his note, he makes as though a crumb stuck in his throat.

Musk   It's no use looking for musk in a dog's kennel.

Mute   They are as mute as fishes.

N

Name A good name is better than riches.

Name A good name keeps its lustre in the dark.

Name Take away my good name, and take away my life.

Nature 'Tis the nature of the beast.

Necessity Necessity knows no law.

Necessity Make a virtue of necessity.

Necessity Necessity is the mother of invention.

Need Need makes the old wife trot.

Need A friend in need is a friend indeed.

Needle To look for a needle in a pottle of hay.

Needy He that's needy when he is marriedShall be rich when he is buried.

Neighbour Love thy neighbour, but pull not down thy hedge.

Neighbour-quart Neighbour-quart is good quart.

Neighbour You must ask your neighbour if you shall live in peace.

Neighbour's House When thy neighbour's house is on fire, be careful of thine own.

Net All is fish that comes to his net.

New Be not the first by whom the new is tried,Be not the last to cast the old aside.

New Broom A new broom sweeps clean.

News No news is good news.

Nimble   A nimble ninepence is better than a slow shilling.

Nip   Nip it in the bud.

Noble   The more noble the more humble.

Nods   The great Homer himself sometimes nods.

Nonsense   A little nonsense now and thenIs relished by the wisest men.

Notice   It is the part of a wise man to take no notice of many things.

Nothing   By doing nothing we learn to do ill.

Nothing   Of nothing comes nothing.

Nothing   Doing nothing is the hardest work.

Nothing   Nothing came out of the sack but what was in it.

Nothing   It is more painful to do nothing than something.

Nothing   Doing nothing is doing ill.

November   November take flail,Let ships no more sail.

Now   Now or never.

Nurse   The nurse's tongue is privileged to talk.

Nutshell   You may as well bid me lade the sea with a nutshell.

O

Oak An oak is not felled by one blow.

Occasion An occasion lost cannot be redeemed.

October Good October, a good blast, To blow the hog acorn and mast.

Offer Never refuse a good offer.

Offender The offender never pardons.

Often Little and often fills the purse.

Old Age When old age is evil, youth can learn no good.

Old Old young, old long.

Old Cat An old cat laps as much as a young kitten.

Old Cock As the old cock crows so crows the young.

Old Dog An old dog barks not in vain.

Old Dog An old dog will learn no tricks.

Older Older and wiser.

Old Fools Old fools are the worst of fools.

Old Foxes Old foxes need no tutors.

Old Friends Old friends to meet, old wine to drink, and old wood to burn.

Old Friends Old friends and old wine are best.

Old Men Old men are twice children.

Old Sack An old sack wanteth much patching.

Old Saws Old saws speak the truth.

Old Sore   It's ill healing an old sore.

Omelettes   You can't make omelettes without breaking eggs.

Once   Once well done is twice done.

One   Make much of one, good men are scarce.

One Hand   One hand will not clasp.

One Hole   The mouse that hath but one hole is easily taken.

One Thing   Too much of one thing is good for nothing.

Opportunity   Opportunity makes the thief.

Opportunity   Opportunity lingers sometimes.

Oppression   Oppression causeth rebellion.

Orderly   In an orderly house all is soon ready.

Orts   Evening orts are good morning fodder.

Otherwise   Some are wise, and some are otherwise.

Ought   Do what thou ought, let come what may.

Outbid   Be not too hasty to outbid another.

Over   Over boots, over shoes.

Overtakes   None is so wise but the fool overtakes him sometimes.

Oysters   Oysters are not good in the month that hath not an R in it.

Own Dog   A man may cause his own dog to bite him.

P

Pain Pain is forgotten where gain follows.

Pain Great pain and little gain make a man soon weary.

Pains No pains, no profit.

Pains Pains are the wages of ill-pleasures.

Painting On painting and fighting look aloof off.

Pardon Pardon all men, but never thyself.

Parents Study to be worthy of your parents.

Partridge If the partridge had the woodcock's thigh,It would be the best bird that ever did fly.

Passion A man in a passion rides a horse that runs away with him.

Patch Patch and sit long, build and soon flit.

Patience Patience is a flower that grows not in every one's garden.

Patience Patience is a plaister for all sores.

Patient As patient as Job.

Pay Pay him in his own coin.

Pay Pay as you go.

Pays Last He that pays last never pays twice.

Payment They who don't intend to pay,Will promise payment any day.

Pearls Cast not pearls before swine.

Peas He who hath most peas may put most in the pot.

Pedlar A small pack suits a small pedlar.

Pedlar Let every pedlar carry his own pack.

Pen Pen and ink are a wit's plough.

Pence Take care of the pence, and the pounds will take care of themselves.

Penny That penny is well spent that saves a groat.

Penny A penny in my purse will bid me drink when all my friends I have will not.

Penny A penny in your pocket is a good companion.

Penny In for a penny, in for a pound.

Penny A penny saved is a penny got.

Penny Wise Penny wise and pound foolish.

Pepper Pepper is black, yet it hath a good smack.

Perch The topmost branch is not the safest perch.

Peril Peril proves who dearly loves.

Perseverance Perseverance kills the game.

Persuasion The persuasion of the fortunate sways the doubtful.

Peter He robs Peter to pay Paul.

Physician Physician heal thyself.

Physicians The best physicians are Doctor Diet, Doctor Cheeriman, and Doctor Quiet.

Pictures Painted pictures are dead speakers.

Pig's Tail You can't make a horn of a pig's tail.

Pillow Sleep on it; the pillow is the best counsellor.

Pilot Every man is a pilot in a calm sea.

Pin He that will not stoop for a pin, shall never be worth a point.

Pin See a pin and let it lie, Want a pin before you die.

Pin A pin a day is a groat a year.

Pinches No one knows where the shoe pinches so well as him who wears it.

Pipe   He can ill pipe that wants his upper lip.

Pitcher   The pitcher does not go so often to the water, but it comes home broken at last.

Pity   Pity, promises, and blame, are always cheap and plentiful.

Pity   Foolish pity spoils a city.

Place   Sit in your place, and none can make you rise.

Place   A place for everything, and everything in its place.

Plain Dealing   Plain dealing's a jewel.

Play   All play and no work,- Gives Tom a ragged shirt.

Play   All work and no play makes Jack a dull boy.

Play   If you play with a fool at home, he'll play with you in the market.

Please All   He that would please all, and himself too,Undertakes what he cannot do.

Pleasing   Pleasing ware is half sold.

Pleasure   Make not a toil of your pleasure.

Plenty   Plenty as blackberries.

Plough   Don't stop the plough to catch a mouse.

Plough   A man must plough with such oxen as he hath.

Plough   He that by the plough would thrive,Himself must either hold or drive.

Poor   Do not live poor to die rich.

Poor   As poor as Job.

Poor Folk   Poor folk have few kindred.

Poor Folk   Poor folk are glad of pottage.

Pope   He that would be Pope must think of nothing else.

Possession   Possession is nine points of the law, and they say there are but ten.

Pot   A little pot is soon hot.

Pot   The pot calls the kettle black.

Poverty   Poverty parts friends.

Poverty Poverty breeds strife.

Poverty Poverty is the mother of health.

Poverty When poverty comes in at the door, friendship leaps out of the window.

Poverty Poverty parteth good fellowship.

Poverty Poverty makes a man acquainted with strange bed-fellows.

Practice Practice makes perfect.

Praise True praise takes root and spreads.

Praise Neither praise nor dispraise thyself, thine actions serve the turn.

Praise Never sound the trumpet of your own praise.

Praise Praise a fair day at night.

Praise Old praise dies, unless you feed it.

Prate Prate is but prate; 'tis money buys land.

Pray He that would learn to pray let him go to sea.

Prettiness Prettiness makes no pottage.

Prettiness Prettiness dies quickly.

Prevention Prevention is better than cure.

Prey Birds of prey do not sing.

Pride Pride feels no pain.

Pride Pride will have a fall.

Pride Pride goes before, and shame follows after.

Procrastination Procrastination is the thief of time.

Promise He is poor indeed that cannot promise nothing.

Promise Be slow to promise, but quick to perform.

Promise Apt to promise, apt to forget.

Promises Promises are too much like pie-crusts, made to be broken.

Proof The proof of the pudding is in the eating.

Prosperity Prosperity gains friends, adversity tries them.

Proud Mind There's nothing agrees worse than a proud mind and a beggar's purse.

Proverb According to the old proverb.

Proverbs Proverbs are the texts of common life.

Pry Pry not into other people's affairs.

Pryeth He that pryeth into every cloud, may be stricken with a thunder-bolt.

Puddle Every path hath a puddle.

Puff Puff not against the wind.

Pull Pull gently on a weak rope.

Pull Down It is easier to pull down than to build.

Punctuality Punctuality begets confidence.

Punishment Many without punishment, none without sin.

Purse Be ruled by your purse.

Purse Let your purse be your master.

Purse You cannot make a purse of a sow's ear.

Purse A full purse maketh the mouth to speak.

Purse He that shows his purse longs to be rid of it.

Purse Be it better or be it worse, Be ruled by him who bears the purse.

Purse A heavy purse makes a light heart.

Purse He who gets four pounds and spends five has no need of a purse.

Purses (wrinkled) Wrinkled purses make wrinkled faces.

Q

Quarrel Don't quarrel with the beggar for his bone.

Quench To cast oil in the fire is not the way to quench it.

Quick Quick at meat, quick at work.

Quietness Next to love, quietness.

Quiet Life Anything for a quiet life.

Quote The devil can quote Scripture to suit his purpose.

R

Ragged Colt A ragged colt may make a good horse.

Rain Rain from east, Two days at least.

Rain Should it rain on Easter Day, There'll be plenty of grass and little hay.

Rain Some rain, some rest.

Rain After rain comes fair weather.

Rain Small rain lays great dust.

Rains It never rains but it pours.

Raise Raise no more spirits than you can conjure down.

Ready Money Ready money will away.

Real Friend He is a real friend who assists one in a pinch.

Reason If we do not hear reason she will one day make herself be heard.

Reason There's reason in roasting of eggs.

Receiver The receiver is as bad as the thief.

Receivers If there were no receivers there would be no thieves.

Reckless Youth Reckless youth makes rueful age.

Reckons He that reckons without his host must reckon again.

Reckoning Fools always come short of their reckoning.

Reckoning Short reckonings make long friends.

Reconcile Reconcile yourself to present trials, the future may bring worse.

Recorder A good recorder sets all in order.

Reigns Man reigns and woman rules.

Reins Men hold the reins, but the women tell them which way to drive.

Religion Better wear a cloak for religion than religion for a cloak.

Remove Remove an old tree and it will wither.

Removed A plant often removed cannot thrive.

Reproof A smart reproof is better than smooth deceit.

Reserve Reserve the master-blow.

Re-Telling A story never loses by re-telling.

Revenge To forget wrong is the greatest revenge.

Revenge Revenge is sweet.

Rich God help the rich, the poor can beg.

Riches Riches are like muck, which stink in a heap, but spread abroad make the earth fruitful.

Riches Riches are but the baggage of fortune.

Ride Better ride on an ass that carries me than a horse that throws me.

Right Hand Let not thy right hand know what thy left hand doeth.

Riseth He that riseth betimes hath something in his head.

River Follow the river and you'll get to the sea.

Road Rich country, bad road.

Roost A bird can roost upon but one branch.

Rolling Stone A rolling stone gathers no moss.

Rome When you are at Rome, do as Rome does.

Rome Rome was not built in a day.

Rudder He that will not be ruled by the rudder must be ruled by the rock.

Rose The fairest rose at last is withered.

Rotten Apple A rotten apple injures its companions.

Rugged Stone A rugged stone grows smooth from hand to hand.

Rule There is no rule without an exception.

Rules Love rules his kingdom without a sword.

Runs He that runs fastest gets the prize.

Runs Fast He that runs fast will not run long.

S

Sack It's a bad sack will abide no clouting.

Sack Nothing comes out of the sack but what was in it.

Saddle Set the saddle on the right horse.

Sadness Sadness and gladness succeed each other.

St. David's Day Upon St. David's day,Put oats and barley in the clay.

St. Stephen Blessed be St. Stephen; There's no fast upon his even.

Sail Make not your sail too large for your ship.

Salmon Salmon and sermon have their season in Lent.

Salt Catch a bird by putting salt on its tail.

Sand You can't make ropes of sand.

Sauce What's sauce for the goose is sauce for the gander.

Sauce Sweet meat must have some sauce.

Save If youth knew what age will crave,It sure would strive to get and save.

Save Who will not save a penny, shall never have many.

Saving Saving is getting.

Saving It's useless saving at the spigot and spending at the bunghole.

Saving Of saving cometh having.

Say Learn to say before you sing.

Saying Saying and doing are two things.

Says If a man says little he thinks the more.

Say Well "Say well," and "do well," end with one letter; To say well, it is well, but to do well is better.

Scabbed Sheep One scabbed sheep infects the whole flock.

Scald Scald not your lips in another man's pottage.

Scalded Cat A scalded cat fears cold water.

Sceptre A sceptre is one thing, a ladle another.

Scholar A mere scholar a mere ass.

Scholars The greatest scholars are not always the wisest men.

Scorning Scorning is catching.

Scotch Mist A Scotch mist will wet an Englishman through to the skin.

Sea On the sea sail; on the land settle.

Season Everything is good in its season.

Season To everything there is a season; and a time to every purpose under heaven.

Second Blow 'Tis the second blow that makes a fray.

Secret He that revealeth his secret maketh himself a slave.

Seeing Seeing is believing.

Seek Seek till you find, and you'll lose no labour.

Seldom Seen Seldom seen, soon forgotten.

Self Self do, self have.

Self Love Self love's a mote in every man's eye.

Self Praise Self praise is no recommendation.

September September blow soft, Till the fruit's in the loft.

Servants Good servants make good masters.

Shadow Catch not at the shadow and lose the substance.

Share Share and share alike.

Shaving It's ill shaving against the wool.

Shear Shear your sheep in May, And shear them all away.

Sheep One sheep follows another.

Ships Ships fear fire more than water.

Shoe The finest shoe often hurts the foot.

Shoe To know where the shoe pinches.

Shoot Every man will shoot at the enemy, but few will go to fetch the shaft.

Shop Keep thy shop, and thy shop will keep thee.

Shorn Sheep God tempers the wind to the shorn sheep.

Short Cuts Short cuts are sometimes longest.

Short Reckonings Short reckonings are soon cleared.

Short and Sweet Short and sweet like a donkey's gallop.

Shrew Every one can tame a shrew but he that hath her.

Sigh Never sigh but send.

Sight Out of sight out of mind.

Silence Silence seldom doth harm.

Silence Silence is consent.

Silence Silence is the best ornament of a woman.

Silver White silver draws black lines.

Silver Spoon He was born with a silver spoon in his mouth.

Sing A bird that can sing and won't sing, must be made to sing.

Sing None but fools and fiddlers sing at their meat.

Sings Who sings drives away care.

Sit Still As good sit still as rise up and fall.

Slander Few people are out of the reach of slander.

Slander Slander leaves a score behind it.

Slavery Account not that work slaveryThat brings in penny savoury.

Sleep   One hour's sleep before midnight is worth two hours after.

Sleeping   There is sleeping enough in the grave.

Sleeping Dog   Don't wake a sleeping dog.

Slip   Better that the feet slip than the tongue.

Sloth   Sloth turneth the edge of wit.

Sloth   Sloth is the mother of poverty.

Slow   Slow and sure.

Sluggard's Guise   The sluggard's guise, Loth to go to bed and loth to rise.

Sluts   Sluts are good enough to make slovens' pottage.

Small Fish   Better are small fish than an empty dish.

Small Things   Small things affect light minds.

Small Things   He that despiseth small things shall fall by little and little.

Smoke   Where there is smoke there is fire.

Snake   Put a snake in your bosom, and when it is warm it will sting you.

Snow   A snow year, a rich year.

Softly   He that goes softly goes surely.

Soft Words   Soft words butter no parsnips.

Soldiers   Soldiers in peace are like chimneys in summer.

Son   My son's my son till he hath got him a wife, But my daughter's my daughter all the days of her life.

Soon Hot   Soon hot, soon cold.

Sooner said   'Tis sooner said than done.

Sorrow   Sorrow and bad weather come unsent for.

Sorrow   Sorrow will pay no debt.

Sorrow   A fat sorrow is better than a lean one.

Sorrow   Sorrow is good for nothing but sin.

Sorrow Sorrow will wear away in time.

Sorrow When sorrow is asleep, wake it not.

Sorrow Sorrow comes unsent for, and, like the unbidden guest, brings his own stool.

Sorrowing He goes a-sorrowing, who goes a-borrowing.

Sound As sound as a nut.

Sour Grapes "Sour grapes," as the fox said when he could not reach them.

Sow Every sow to her own trough.

Sows Who sows in May gets little that way.

Sows What a man sows, that shall he also reap.

Spare 'Tis too late, to spare when the bottom is bare.

Spare It is better to spare at the brim than the bottom.

Spare Spare when young and spend when old.

Spare Spare to speak and spare to spend.

Speak There is a time to speak as well as to be silent.

Speak Speak well of the dead.

Speak Many speak much that cannot speak well.

Speak Speak fair and think what you will.

Speaks He that speaks me fair and loves me not, I'll speak him fair and trust him not.

Speculation Speculation completes what extravagance began.

Speech Speech is the picture of the mind.

Spend Spend not where you may save; spare not where you must spend.

Spend Carefully spend, and God will send.

Spend Spend and be free, but make no waste.

Spender To a good spender God is the treasurer.

Spenders Great spenders are bad lenders.

Spends   He who more than his worth doth spend, Makes a rope his life to end; He who spends more than he should, Shall not have to spend when he would.

Spends   You may know by a penny how a shilling spends.

Spendthrift   It is the thrift of a spendthrift which ruins him most effectually.

Spice   Who hath spice enough may season his meat as he pleaseth.

Spite   Don't cut your nose off to spite your face.

Spits   Who spits against the wind spits in his own face.

Split   He would split a hair.

Spoil   Too many cooks spoil the broth.

Spoil   Spoil not the ship for a penn'orth of tar.

Spoken of   Better be ill spoken of by one before all, than by all before one.

Sport   It's poor sport that is not worth the candle.

Sport   No sport, no pie.

Spots   Rich men's spots are covered with money.

Sprat   Throw a sprat to catch a whale.

Spur   Do not spur a free horse.

Stable   Being born in a stable does not make a man a horse.

Stake   An ill stake standeth longest.

Standers by   Standers by see more than the gamesters.

Standing   The higher the standing the lower the fall.

Standing Pools   Standing pools gather filth.

Stars   Stars are not seen during sunshine.

Starve   He would starve in a cook-shop.

Steal   He that will steal an egg will steal an ox.

Steal   He that will steal a pin will steal a better thing.

Steal One man may better steal a horse than another look over the hedge.

Steed When the steed is stolen the stable door shall be shut.

Step by Step Step by step the ladder is climbed.

Sticks Little sticks kindle the fire, but great ones put it out.

Stile He that will not go over the stile must be thrust through the gate.

Still Water Trust not still water nor a silent man.

Still Water Keep me from still water; from that which is rough I can keep myself.

Still Waters Still waters run deep.

Stinking Fish Never cry "Stinking fish."

Stitch A stitch in time saves nine.

Stock Whoso lacketh a stock, his gain's not worth a chip.

Stolen Kisses Stolen kisses are sweet.

Stomach The full stomach loatheth the honeycomb, but to the hungry every bitter thing is sweet.

Stomach With stomach, wife, and conscience keep on good terms.

Stone Wall Hard upon hard makes a bad stone wall;But soft upon soft makes none at all.

Stools Between two stools he comes to the ground.

Stoop He must stoop that hath a low door.

Storm After a storm comes a calm.

Store Store is no sore.

Story One story is good until another's told.

Straight Trees Straight trees have crooked roots.

Stratagem By stratagem, not valour.

Stream No striving against the stream.

Strife Weight and measure take away strife.

Strife Haste makes waste, and waste makes want, and want makes strife between the good man and his wife.

Strike Strike while the iron is hot.

Strokes Little strokes fell great oaks.

Study Morning is the time for study.

Stumbles He that runs in the night stumbles.

Stumbles He that stumbles twice over the same stone, deserves to break his shins.

Stumbles 'Tis a good horse that never stumbles, and a good wife that never grumbles.

Subjects' Love The subjects' love is the king's lifeguard.

Success Nothing succeeds like success.

Success 'Tis not in mortals to command success,But we'll do more, Sempronius, we'll deserve it.

Suckers The young suckers drain the old tree.

Sufferance Of sufferance comes ease.

Sufficient Sufficient for the day is the evil thereof.

Suit That suit is best that best fits me.

Sunshine No sunshine but hath some shadow.

Supperless Better go to bed supperless than to rise in debt.

Suppers Light suppers make long lives.

Sure Sure bind, sure find.

Surgeon A good surgeon must have an eagle's eye, a lion's heart, and a lady's hand.

Swallow One swallow does not make a summer.

Swallow One swallow makes not a spring, nor one woodcock a winter.

Sweat No sweat, no sweet.

Sweep Sweep before your own door.

Sweep They have need of a besom that sweep the house with a turf.

Sweet He deserves not the sweet that will not taste the sour.

Swim He must needs swim that's held up by the chin.

Swim Never trust yourself out of your depth till you can swim.

Sword He that strikes with the sword shall be beaten with the scabbard.

Sword Who draws his sword against his prince must throw away the scabbard.

T

Table A poor man's table is soon spread.

Table Who depends upon another man's table often dines late.

Tale-Bearer Remove the tale-bearer and contention ceaseth.

Tale-Bearers Put no faith in tale-bearers.

Talk Talk of the devil and his imp appears.

Talkers The greatest talkers are always the least doers.

Talking Talking pays no toll.

Taste To him that hath lost his taste, sweet is sour.

Teacheth He teacheth ill who teacheth all.

Tears Nothing dries up sooner than tears.

Teeth A man may dig his grave with his teeth.

Temperance Temperance is the best physic.

Tempter The tempter is the greater rogue.

Thanks He loseth his thanks who promiseth and delayeth.

Thatched When I have thatched his house he would throw me down.

Thief Give a thief rope enough and he'll hang himself.

Thief The thief's sorry because he is caught, not because he is the thief.

Thief Set a thief to take a thief.

Thieves All are not thieves that dogs bark at.

Think One may think that dares not speak.

Think Think twice before you speak once.

Think Think much, speak little, and write less.

Think Who thinks to live must live to think,Else mind and body lose their link.

Thinks The horse thinks one thing, and he that rides him another.

Thinkers Thinkers govern toilers.

Thistles Gather thistles, expect prickles.

Thistles He that sows nothing plants thistles.

Thorn No rose without a thorn.

Thorn The thorn comes forth with his point forwards.

Thorns Roses, mind you, have thorns.

Thorns He that handles thorns shall prick his fingers.

Thoughts Second thoughts are best.

Thoughts Thoughts are free.

Threatened There are more threatened than struck.

Threepence If you make not much of threepence you'll ne'er be worth a groat.

Thrifty Thrifty men are fond of thrifty sayings.

Thrive He that will thrive must rise at five.He that hath thriven may lie till seven.

Thunder Thunder in December foretells fine weather.

Thunders When it thunders the thief becomes honest.

Thyself For what thou canst do thyself rely not on another.

Tide There is a tide in the affairs of man which, taken at the flood, leads on to fortune.

Tide Every tide has its ebb.

Tide The tide will fetch away what the ebb brings.

Time Take time by the forelock.

Time A mouse, in time, may bite in two a cable.

Time Take time when time is, for time will away.

Time Time and tide tarry for no man.

Time Time assuages the greatest grief.

Time Time cures sorrow.

Time Time is the rider that breaks youth.

Time Time tries all.

Timely Timely blossom timely ripe.

Title Simon Noland, clown, is a better style and title than Humphrey Hadland, gent.

To-day To-day me, to-morrow thee.

Tom He's Tom Tell-troth.

To-morrow To-morrow comes never.

Tongue A man may hold his tongue in an ill time.

Tongue Temper the tongue.

Tongue Confine your tongue, lest it confine you.

Tongue Keep your tongue within your teeth.

Tongue The tongue breaketh bone, Though itself have none.

Tongue The tongue's not steel, yet it cuts.

Tongue The tongue talks at the head's cost.

Tongue One tongue is enough for a woman.

Tongue Who has not a good tongue, ought to have good hands.

Too Late Better three hours too soon than a minute too late.

Tools A bad workman quarrels with his tools.

Tools What is a workman without his tools?

Too Far Too far east is west.

Too Much He that grasps at too much, holds fast nothing.

Top Sawyers We can't all be top sawyers.

Trade He that hath a trade hath an estate.

Trade Every man to his trade.

Trade Trade knows neither friends nor kindred.

Trade Trade is the mother of money.

Trades Jack of all trades, and master of none.

Tradesman A tradesman who gets not loseth.

Travels He that travels far knows much.

Tree A tree is known by its fruit, and not by its leaves.

Tree Remove an old tree and it will wither to death.

Trees Set trees poor, and they will grow rich; set them rich, and they will grow poor.

Trees You cannot see wood for trees.

Trifle Fall not out with a friend for a trifle.

Trouble He who seeketh trouble never misseth it.

Troubled Waters Never fish in troubled waters.

Troubles Never make troubles of trifles.

Troubles Hidden troubles disquiet most.

True Word There's many a true word spoken in jest.

True That is true which all men say.

Trust If you trust before you try, You may repent it ere you die.

Trust Trust in God, and keep your powder dry.

Trust Not Trust not a broken staff.

Trust Not Trust not a horse's heel, nor a dog's tooth.

Truth Truth lies in a well.

Truth Truth is stranger than fiction.

Truth Fair fall truth and daylight.

Truth Speak the truth and shame the devil.

Truth Truth hath a good face, but bad clothes.

Truth Truth may be blamed, but it can't be shamed.

Truth Whatever you do, whatever you say, Tell your doctor and lawyer the truth alway.

Try Try your friend before you trust him.

Tub Every tub must stand on its own bottom.

Turn One good turn deserves another.

Turned Swine, women, and bees are not to be turned.

Twelfth Day At twelfth-day the days are lengthened a cock's stride.

Twenty As good twenty as nineteen.

Twice If things were to be done twice, all would be wise.

Two Faces Never carry two faces under one hat.

Two Heads Two heads are better than one.

Two Places One cannot be in two places at once.

Two Sundays When two Sundays come in one week—that is, never.

U

Unhappy An unhappy lad may make a good man.

Units The greatest number is made up of units.

Unknown Unknown, unmissed.

Unminded Unminded, unmoaned.

Untaught Better untaught than ill-taught.

Use Use is second nature.

Use Use the means, and God will give the blessing.

Utility Utility is preferable to grandeur.

V

Valentine's Day On Valentine's day will a good goose lay, If she be a good goose, her dame well to pay, She will lay two eggs before Valentine's day.

Valley He who stays in the valley will never get over the hill.

Valour Valour can do little without discretion.

Valour Valour that parleys is near yielding.

Venture Nothing venture nothing win.

Venture Venture a small fish to catch a great one.

Venture Venture not all in one ship.

Very Last Fools think themselves wise to the very last.

Vicar of Bray The vicar of Bray will be vicar of Bray still.

Vice Vice is nourished by being concealed.

Vine Make the vine poor, and it will make you rich.

Vinegar The sweetest wine makes the sharpest vinegar.

Virtues Search others for their virtues, thyself for their faults.

Vows Vows made in storms are forgotten in calms.

W

Wager A wager is a fool's argument.

Wages He who serves well need not be afraid to ask his wages.

Waits He that waits on another man's trencher, makes many a late dinner.

Want The worth of a thing is best known by the want of it.

Want of For want of a nail the shoe is lost; for want of a shoe the horse is lost; for want of a horse the rider is lost.

War War, hunting, and law, are as full of trouble as pleasure.

War War is death's feast.

War Who preacheth war is the devil's chaplain.

War (good) He that makes a good war makes a good peace.

War (good) Good wares make quick markets.

Warm He that is warm thinks all are so.

Warm He is wise enough that can keep himself warm in winter.

Warm The head and feet kept warm,The rest will take no harm.

Washing There's no washing the blackamore white.

Waste Waste not, want not.

Waste Wilful waste makes woeful want.

Watch Good watch prevents misfortune.

Watch You may be a wise man though you cannot make a watch.

Watched Pot A watched pot never boils.

Water Water bewitched.

Water We never know the worth of water till the well is dry.

Wax He that hath a head of wax must not walk in the sun.

Way Where there's a will there's a way.

Ways (more) There are more ways to kill a dog than hanging.

Ways To him that wills ways are not wanting.

Weakest Let the weakest go to the wall.

Weakest Where it is weakest there the thread breaketh.

Wealth Their folly pleads the privilege of wealth.

Wearer The wearer best knows where the shoe pinches.

Wearing Everything is the worse for wearing.

Wears Constant dropping wears the stone.

Weather 'Tis pity fair weather should do any harm.

Weather (change) Any flat can talk of change of weather.

Wedding Wedding and ill-wintering tame both man and beast.

Wedlock Wedlock is a padlock.

Weds Who weds ere he be wise shall die ere he thrive.

Weep As great a pity to see a woman weep, as to see a goose go barefoot.

Welcome As welcome as the flowers in May.

Welcome "Welcome death," quoth the rat, when the trap fell down.

Welcome Welcome is the best dish on the table.

Well Let well alone.

Well When the well is dug it is easy enough to pump.

Well-Doing Be not weary of well-doing.

Well-Ordered All things are soon prepared in a well-ordered house.

Wells Well-drawn wells give the sweetest water.

Wept I wept when I was born, and every day shows why.

Whet A whet is no let [hindrance].

Whistle You may pay too dear for your whistle.

Why There's ne'er a why, but there's a wherefore.

Wide Wide will wear but narrow will tear.

Wife Choose your wife on Saturday, and not on a Sunday.

Wife He that goes far from home for a wife, either intends to cheat or will be cheated.

Wife A man's best fortune or his worst is his wife.

Wife There is one good wife in the country, and every man thinks he hath her.

Wife (good) A good wife makes a good husband.

Wife (good) A good wife and healthAre a man's best wealth.

Wife (good) Saith Solomon the wiseA good wife's a prize.

Wife (news) He that tells his wife news is but newly married.

Wild Oats Happy is he who hath sown his wild oats betimes.

Wiles Wise men are not caught by wiles.

Wilful If wilful will to water, wilful must be drowned.

Wilful Man A wilful man never wants woe.

Will Take the will for the deed.

Will They that cannot do as they will, must do as they can.

Will Will without reason is blind.

Will Not If one will not, another will.

Will (ready) Where the will is ready, the feet are light.

Will (way) Where there's a will there's a way.

Willing Horse All lay load on the willing horse.

Willing Mind Nothing is impossible to a willing mind.

Willows Willows are weak, yet they bend other wood.

Win Win first, lose last.

Wind (north) When the wind's in the northYou need not go forth [*to fish*].

Wind (east) When the wind's in the eastThe fish will bite least.

Wind (south) When the wind's in the southThe bait goes in their mouth.

Wind (west) When the wind's in the west The fish will bite best.

Wind Where the wind is on Candlemas Day There it will stick to the end of May.

Wind (east) When the wind is in the east,'Tis neither good for man nor beast.

Wind (ill) It's an ill wind that blows nobody good.

Wind (south) When the wind's in the southIt's in the rain's mouth.

Wind (still) No weather is illIf the wind be still.

Windfalls None ever yet got fat on windfalls.

Windfalls You cannot drive a windmill with a pair of bellows.

Wine More have been drowned in wine than water.

Wine When wine sinks, words swim.

Wine Wine is the master's, but the goodness is the drawer's.

Wine (good) Good wine needs no bush.

Wine (in) When wine is in, wit is out.

Wine (turncoat) Wine is a turncoat, first a friend, then an enemy.

Wink Wink at small faults.

Wink A wink's as good as a nod to a blind horse.

Winter (good) A good winter brings a good summer.

Winter Winter finds out what summer lays up.

Wisdom By wisdom peace, by peace plenty.

Wisdom The fear of the Lord is the beginning of wisdom.

Wisdom Wisdom rides upon the ruins of folly.

Wise Better wise than wealthy.

Wise Men Wise men care not for what they cannot have.

Wishes If wishes were horses, beggars would ride.

Wishes If wishes were thrushes, beggars would eat birds.

Wishes If wishes would bide, beggars would ride.

Wishes If wishes were butter-cakes, beggars would bite.

Wit Wit is the lightning of the mind.

Wit Wit bought is twice taught.

Wit You may truss up all his wit in an egg-shell.

Wit Wit ill applied is a dangerous weapon.

Wit Wit is folly, unless a wise man hath the keeping of it.

Wit Wit may be bought too dear.

Wits He that lives upon his wits, breaks for want of stock.

Wive A man cannot both wive and thrive in a year.

Woe Woe follows wickedness.

Wolf He had enough to keep the wolf from the door.

Wolves Wolves lose their teeth, but not their memory.

Woman's Strength A woman's strength is in her tongue.

Woman's Work A woman's work is never at an end.

Women Discreet women have neither eyes nor ears.

Women (wills) Women must have their wills while they live, because they make none when they die.

Wonder A wonder lasts but nine days.

Woo To woo is a pleasure in young men, a fault in old.

Woodcock One woodcock does not make a winter.

Wooing Happy is the wooing,That is not long a-doing.

Wool Many go for wool and come back shorn.

Wool Sellers Wool sellers know wool buyers.

Word An honest man's word is as good as his bond.

Words A man of words and not of deeds,Is like a garden full of weeds.

Words Words are but sands,'Tis money buys lands.

Words Sometimes words Wound more than swords.

Words Words are like weights, gravity gives them effect.

Words Words are for women, actions for men.

Words and Blows Words are but wind, But blows unkind.

Word (enough) A word is enough to the wise.

Words (evening) Words spoken in an evening the wind carrieth away.

Words (fair) Fair words butter no parsnips.

Words (fair) Fair words will not keep a cat from starving.

Words (few) Few words are best.

Words (good) Good words cool more than cold water.

Words (good) Good words fill not a sack.

Words (many) Many words will not fill a bushel.

Words (soft) Soft words hurt not the mouth.

Work They that will not work in heat, must hunger in frost.

Workmen (bad) Bad workmen always complain of their tools.

World One half of the world knows not how the other half lives.

World The world is his who knows how to wait for it.

World The world was never so dull but if one won't another will.

World This world is nothing except it tend to the next.

World's Pulse There needs a long time to know the world's pulse.

Worm Tread on a worm and it will turn.

Worst When things get to the worst, they'll mend.

Worst Spoke The worst spoke in the cart-wheel breaks first.

Would "He that wolde not when he might, He shall not when he wold-a."

Wounds Wounds may heal, but not those made by ill words.

Wranglers Wranglers never want words.

Wrath A soft answer turneth away wrath.

Wrestle He that is thrown would ever wrestle.

Wretch He who maketh others wretched is himself a wretch, whether prince or peasant.

Wrongs Two wrongs will not make a right.

Wrong Sow To take the wrong sow by the ear.

Y

Year Say no ill of the year till it is passed.

Years Years know more than books.

Yes and No Between a woman's yes and no,There is not room for a pin to go.

Yorkshire Yorkshire fashion—every man pay his share.

Young Old young, and old long.

Yourself Help yourself and your friends will like you.

Yourself If you want a thing done, do it yourself.

Youth A growing youth hath a wolf in his stomach.

Youth If youth knew what age would crave.It would both get and save.

Youth Youth and white paper take any impression.

Youth Youth will have its swing.

Yule Yule is good on Yule even.

Z

Zeal Zeal without knowledge is fire without light.

Zeal Zeal without knowledge is the sister of folly.

Zeal Zeal without knowledge is frenzy.

Made in the USA
Monee, IL
07 July 2026